READING
FOR
PLEASURE

MICHAEL ROSEN

A child
A book
A read
A chat.
This is the way
the mind grows.

Not with a test
but a tale.

Introduction

This is a booklet for you to use, discuss, adapt and change according to your needs in schools. It's the fourth in my series of self-published booklets and overlaps and adds to what they say.

Reading for pleasure is both obvious and obscure at the same time. By being called 'for pleasure' it sounds as if it might be trivial or some kind of add-on or extra. We know from all the research (which you can find very easily on line) that when children read widely and often they can access the curriculum much more easily, which leads in crude terms to higher scores in tests and exams. Nothing wrong with that! However, it does much more than that. Of course it does. Reading widely and often opens up worlds beyond a child's own experience. It enables a child to access ways of thinking that the strategies and approaches of writing create in the minds of readers: various kinds of abstract and logical thought that are embedded in sentences, paragraphs, sequences of writing across several pages, chapters and whole books. Far from being an add-on, these are central to what education is about.

When it comes to fiction, we invite readers to discover ideas and feelings attached to beings we come to care about. Fiction combines ideas and feelings. It entangles ideas about, say, right and wrong, with how we feel about the characters that are put in front of us. We ask ourselves whether it was right or fair for that character to have done that? We ask questions about how people come to behave in ways we might think of as wrong. Our feelings towards these characters are entangled with these broader ideas to do with values, beliefs, and, as I say, ideas. Part of the fun of book-chat, talk about books is that we can discuss these things. This is the power of interpretation – a much wider and more significant matter than that of 'retrieval' and 'inference' as dictated by the tests. It is through interpretation that we engage with ideas and, I would argue, with the 'stuff that matters'. The retrieval-inference model of reading treats books, stories, texts as if they are egg-boxes with a defined number of eggs in them. The task of the reader or test-candidate is supposedly to get the eggs out – at which point the egg-box is empty. All its meaning and purpose has been taken out. Interpretation treats texts as never-ending strings of meaning that can go on and on being taken from texts. Put another way, when writers write, we don't do it in order to close off meaning as one definite thing. We do it in order to open up conversations in people's minds or between people so that things can be chewed over, thought about, and, as is often said, 'resonate' or 'chime' with that person's experience and life. Writers are 'provocateurs'. We want to provoke thought and chat so that people can find ideas, feelings and – perhaps – wisdom! This booklet is written in that tradition.

In my other booklets and books I've written out a little sequence of questions which I suggest are ways in which talk about books, book-chat, reading for pleasure and the like are enabled and encouraged. Again, I offer these for you to adapt and change as you see fit.

Is there anything, any scene (or a particular scene) that makes you think of something that has happened to you or to someone you know? What was this? Why or how does the scene in the book make you think of the thing that happened to you? What's similar about it? What's different? (This question enables children to engage with analogies between life and the book. Analogies are the basis for abstract thought. Analogies are how we begin to make categories. Depending on the age of child, we can help them do this and form categories of e.g., 'anger' or 'pity' or 'sadness'.

Is there any part or scene or the whole book which made you think of something else that you've read or seen in a film or TV programme? What was it? Why or how did you think of this as similar? (This question enables children to see how 'texts' are not alone in the world but are linked to other texts through how they are told, or the scenes or the 'motifs' or the kinds of feelings they engender. This is called 'intertextuality' and in a way we read with our intertextuality along with our experience of life as lived. We read with the texts we already know – wherever they are from: books, TV, films, games, or wherever. Again, when children start to talk about these, we can start to create categories, or even abstract thought about groups of similar ideas or feelings.)

Are there any questions you would like to ask the author? Who would like to be the author? Let's ask the 'author' these questions. If the 'author' can't answer them, are there places we can look to find out if that will help us? (e.g., the author's website? Or a book about the author?). Are there any questions you would like to ask a character in the book? We can freeze-frame a scene and ask a character to tell us what he or she is thinking at this precise moment (hot-seating). Why are you thinking this? Or we can just talk about possible ways of thinking and talking that a character might have in answer to questions we have for that character. (These questions generated in a group will enable us to access meanings, ideas and feelings that are expressed in a book. We can always feed into this talk or follow this talk with information, knowledge, categories, terminology that we,as teachers and adults have. This kind of free exploration does not preclude the kinds of knowledge that are required by the curriculum or the exams. It's a bridge to it, if needed or necessary.)

This little cluster of questions might be preceded with something more general to do with feelings: e.g., is there any part of this 'text' (book etc.) which 'affected' you, that you were 'moved by' or 'scared by' or 'made happy by'. If this is the first question, then it can be a way for the whole conversation about the book or story to start off with 'feelings'. Some teachers have told me that they've found that this is the best place to start, rather than with the ones above. They have got to those questions next.

This booklet is far from being the only source of information out there about reading for pleasure. You'll find websites and resources in the chapters and in my other booklets. In this introduction, though, may I draw your attention to one developed by the writer Alan Gibbons in conjunction with what was the NUT and is now the NEU. You'll find it here:

www.teachers.org.uk/reading-for-pleasure

Remember: the more you share and talk about these things, the more the children will get out of it.

Part 1

A 20-Point Plan for Reading

'If we don't learn to love reading, we won't read very much. And if we don't read widely and often, we miss out on the ideas and feelings that are expressed through writing.'

What follows are 20 suggestions for how to encourage reading-for-pleasure in schools. They are not a list of instructions. They are for you to adapt and change according to your circumstances.

Can I suggest that the best way to use them is for a group of teachers – or the whole staff – take them and any other such blueprints on reading for pleasure and thrash out a policy for yourselves?

1. Improve home-school liaison

It's really important to share the idea that books and talking about books really matters, but this can be difficult to extend beyond the classroom into the home environment. A good starting point is to have someone in each year group who is responsible for talking with individual parents or carers about their child's reading. The discussion should be very specific and matched to the interests of each child and their parents or carers. Talk about particular books, magazines or reading websites, about your local library or book clubs that might be of interest. Make sure the dialogue is ongoing, not a one-off chat! It may be a good idea to set up some kind of parents' committee to expand this. If we bear in mind that one of the purposes of reading for pleasure is to reach those children who are the least likely to read widely and often, then we may well find that we need to do all we can to enlist the help of parents who themselves feel wary about books.

2. Hold events

Arrange for writers, illustrators, storytellers, librarians and book enthusiasts of all kinds to visit your school regularly to talk about books and perform to your children. Some events – such as a special story telling assembly or a local author visit – won't take much time to organise and will help your school become a place where everyone talks about books and reading. Or why not pull out all the stops to create a real splash once a term? How about a launch event for the first day of your campaign to inspire everyone? Then you can ask the children and their parents for ideas about what kind of reading event they'd like to hold next!

When you invite an author in, please spend at least a fortnight looking at the author's work and life. This means that the children learn about what it means to write. It widens their sense of what it means to make books. Try to spend time imitating how the writer writes e.g., an opening for a book, or how the writer wrote jokes or created tension, or wrote a particular kind of scene. You can invite people who are passionate about reading into school, but there are bound to be lots of book enthusiasts in school already among your staff, parents, carers and older pupils! You could designate them as Reading Buddies for the younger or more reluctant readers to spread their enthusiasm for reading across the whole school. There are some excellent ground rules for Reading Buddies at:
www.readingrevolution.co.uk/get-started.

3. Create close links with booksellers

If you are lucky enough to have a local bookseller, forge and maintain good contacts with booksellers as they can often help you find writers and storytellers to visit your school. Don't limit yourself to the syndicated book fair contact; talk to your local and specialist bookshops too. If there is a children's section in your local bookshop the shop manager will have a good overview of what's available for children, will be knowledgeable about authors and illustrators and will probably be used to organising author visits to schools and setting up bookstalls to sell copies of suitable books at the same time.

Spread the word about your local bookshop – many good booksellers run regular weekend storytelling sessions with local and well-known authors. Keep up to date with their events so that you can let the children know when something good is coming up.

4. Appoint a school librarian – or share one between schools

If you don't have one already, setting up a school library takes time and commitment and keeping it running in a way that continues to inspire children requires the dedication and skill of someone who is trained and interested in the job. If this seems like too big a task, start small with a mini library in every classroom. Not enough space? Make room! If the library is hidden away, books may become sidelined so why not think about using a corner of your school hall or another space that gets lots of traffic?

Not enough in-school expertise? Bring it in! Ask your local librarian to come into school to help you set up the kind of library that suits your needs. Not enough time? Find a volunteer! If you ask, you might find a parent or better still, two parents, who can support the teachers and perhaps eventually take on the job themselves. Once you have your library, however small, make sure you find time for the children to use it regularly. Keep it fresh, think of new ideas to make it an interesting or exciting place to go to.

5. Set up school book clubs

Aim to have an active book club that includes every teacher and every child in every class. Conduct a survey and ask everyone what kind of club they want. To appeal to everyone, you might need to set up more than one club. Work with your school librarian and other book enthusiasts to organise the appropriate books and to ensure everything runs smoothly. You can ask the children to help promote the club/s and cover some of your literacy objectives at the same time by challenging them to design posters to advertise them. Make sure you refresh book club books regularly to generate wide-ranging and in-depth conversations about reading.

6. Share information on local libraries

Aim to make every family in the school aware of where the local library is, when it's open and what's available there for children. Arrange trips to the library in school time, planning the visit ahead by liaising with the local librarian. Make visits to the local library appealing by creating an exciting information pack for your children to take home and read with their parents or carers. Include your school logo, photographs, artwork and quotes from pupils and parents who love reading, saying how brilliant particular sections of the library are or why a particular event at the library was so inspiring.

7. Adopt an author or illustrator

See the Patron of Reading scheme: www.patronofreading.co.uk

If you can, work with an author or illustrator (ideally both!) for an extended period of time. This is a great way to achieve some of your literacy objectives about understanding an author's work in more depth. To find the right author for your school, first decide what you want to achieve. If you have a theme that's running for a term or a year that you'd like to tie in with, look for an author who has written in this area. Visit www.societyofauthors.org or www.booktrust.org.uk to find an author that fits the bill.

8. Try book-making

Making hand-made books needs lots of pairs of hands. Depending on the techniques you use, book making can include cutting, hole-punching, sticking, stapling, sewing, using the computer . . . Don't be shy about asking parents and carers if they have a free hour to come into support the practical sessions. Then show off your hand-made books! Set up a display in the school foyer. Bring out the books and celebrate the children's achievements at parents' evenings and invite each class to take it in turn to hold up their hand-made books in assembly for all to see. For practical ideas on making books, take a look at www.makingbooks.com/freeprojects.shtml.

9. Share books

Sharing books and encouraging conversations about them is crucial to keep reading enjoyment alive. Try to build time into the school day for book swaps and assembly presentations of 'this week's good read' or book posters and display book reviews prominently around school. Survey pupils or use the suggestion box to find your own ideas for the best way to share books in school. And don't forget to get your keen readers involved. They will have a good idea about which books might interest more reluctant children so pair them up as Reading Buddies.

10. Read widely

School trips or events at school are an ideal opportunity to encourage your children to read more widely. Find books for children to read that are relevant to the trip or event's theme. Ask your school librarian to check if you have relevant books in school or ask the local librarian to suggest books you can borrow. Send a letter home with children asking families to bring in relevant books and other literature to share and involve the staff too. Wherever you go on a school visit, see if you can collect the leaflets or booklets that are given away or on sale at the site. Bring these back and display them in the class for the children to browse.

11. Try regular themed activities

Make sure you incorporate books whenever there is themed activity at school. Arrange for each class to visit your local library to search for books to support your theme and ask children to bring in magazines, pictures and other reading material from home. Reading of all kinds, in all genres and for all ages can be covered by these activities, but you don't need to do everything at once. If you have an active and varied programme throughout the school year, you will have covered a lot of ground by the end of each term and you can even follow up term-time themed activities with reading challenges for the holidays! Think of a theme as having a 'cluster' of books or other reading matter which 'surround' the theme. This widens and enriches the subject in hand and allows the children to wander off into related areas. If you have a School Library Service in your area, they can do this for you.

This site may be useful for you: www.booksfortopics.com

12. Get the reading habit

Spending time on books and reading in school will show children how important books are and will really help your pupils to see them in new and imaginative ways. Develop a whole-school policy about reading books out loud every day and remember, assembly is a great time to promote reading. Encourage children to chat about the books they are reading. Every angle and approach to book chat is valid and this is particularly true for reluctant readers. Give children time to read a book in school every day. Don't give them excerpts that can be fitted into 15 minutes, but instead, give them 15 minutes to read what will eventually be a whole book and get Reading Buddies to support the reluctant readers. Encourage parents and carers to keep reading to their children. Run a survey asking every child in school to name the author and title of three books they've read recently then challenge them to review their favourite books. There is no need to get hung up on children having to read books that are supposedly age-appropriate. There are, for example, some challenging and controversial picture books that are great for older children.

13. Collect odd, old books

Make reading intriguing by finding a place for old or strange books in your school. Have exciting, ever-changing, even weird books to provoke ideas and conversation in the Headteacher's office and on every teacher's desk. Visit your local charity or second-hand bookshop and search out books with leather or cloth bindings and different styles of lettering, such as gold blocking. Display old posters to show what book promotions used to look like and experiment with tea-staining to make display lettering look aged. You could even organise a book treasure hunt! Hide books around the school, ideally hiding each book in a particularly relevant spot. Maybe the name of the author could reference an object in school or the content of the story could link to a particular teacher or room in the school? Use the internet to show the children e.g., an illuminated manuscript of the Bible or what an old children's book used to look like. The British Library site has hundreds of digitized books now, including many old children's books.

14. Keep and use book reviews

Get into the habit of regularly cutting out and keeping (or cutting and pasting) reviews of children's books. Get all members of staff involved so you are all informed about which new books are coming out, why they are good and how they might link to ongoing work and discussions in school. Keep the best and more relevant reviews in an accessible place and introduce a system of adding to and actively sharing the reviews with your colleagues – perhaps by making them the subject of a monthly staff training session. Put some of these up on a notice-board in your class. There are regular book reviews of children's books in 'Books for Keeps' (online), *Carousel* (a magazine for parents, teachers and librarians), *Sunday Times*, *Guardian*, *Observer*. There are websites now to help parents and children find their way to books, some with children's reviews e.g.:

www.lovemybooks.co.uk
www.lovereading.co.uk
www.lovereading4kids.co.uk
www.thereadingrealm.co.uk

15. Avoid reading being 'squeezed out'

Finding time in the day for free reading as well as for discussions about reading can be difficult. To avoid it being squeezed out by other things, establish a principle that in gaps – such as waiting for a visitor or when the projector is being set up – children can get out their reading books or talk about their books together. Support this principle by showing a keen interest in the book each child is reading, encourage discussion by asking open-ended questions and group the children in different ways to chat about their books. Have your own book to read alongside the children and chat about it in an excited way too.

16. Have plenty of books around in meetings

Always make sure there are plenty of wonderful children's books in the room when a meeting about literacy is taking place. This is particularly important when teachers are helping parents and carers to understand literacy and the importance of regularly reading with their children. There are great lists of recommended children's books at www.booktrust.org.uk

17. Encourage varied reading

Ensure all your children are excited by reading by providing a variety of reading materials to suit their various interests. As well as giving children opportunities to enjoy classic stories at school, include annuals and football programmes open at the Junior Supporters pages, and books that tie in with TV shows and films. Place a book basket in the school foyer to catch children's eyes as they enter the building and include information about how the books can be borrowed, making sure the process is easy so that budding reading enthusiasts aren't put off at the first hurdle. Display the books in school face-out, so that the bright cover illustrations and graphics catch children's attention as well as tell them what's inside. To help you be diverse with children's books, please try: www.letterboxlibrary.com

18. Perform stories

Performance is a great way to engage children in the excitement of stories but you don't need to limit it to the children. Wrap up curriculum evenings or group meetings with parents and carers with a read-aloud session from a children's book, choosing stories that are well-suited to being read aloud such as one of Julia Donaldson's and Axel Sheffler's masterpieces. Encourage parents to be vocal by leading by example and aim for all staff to agree up front that they too will join in.

19. Share precious books

Establish a school culture that values the sharing of favourite books from childhood and you will uncover some fascinating stories. Start with your own favourites to get the ball rolling and encourage all staff (including non-teaching staff) , parents, grandparents and other carers to share their memories of favourite books from their childhoods. Ask them to bring in and show off the books that they have kept since they were children. Time and inspiration permitting, you could turn the gathered memories into projects that support your curriculum objectives in an enjoyable way.

20. Train colleagues on children's literature

Aim to be clear and vocal about your support for specific instruction on children's literature to be once again included in teacher and assistant training courses. Talk to colleagues about what you, as a school, would change about the present system and lobby relevant organisations to help make it happen.

Teresa Cremin from the Open University has years of research and practice which shows that one key way (if not, the key way) for reading for pleasure to take off in your school is for teachers to become interested readers of children's books. She sets up groups all round the country to encourage this. I cannot recommend this highly enough. You can look into her work here:

www.researchrichpedagogies.org/research/team/reading-for-pleasure

Reading For Pleasure Action Plan

The next few pages illustrate how one school adapted my plan and made it work for them. Thanks to Ian Eagleton for sharing with me.

Reading For Pleasure Action Plan

Objective	Strategies	Responsible	Evaluate	Feedback and notes on progress
Develop library space – appoint a class librarian/ develop use of library space at lunchtime	Classes to appoint a class librarian, who is responsible for representing the class in a weekly meeting and running the library sessions. Could also ask interested children to apply for position? Enquire about parent helper, trained librarian? Cost of library system?	Class teacher English Lead SLT Termly	Class teachers to monitor use of library and enforce responsibilities of librarian. Librarians able to recommend books. Attractive and inviting library space. Timetable for use?	Spoken to PTA about funding. Some furniture and rugs purchased from IKEA. Parent helpers approached about sorting library – very messy!

Objective	Strategies	Responsible	Evaluate	Feedback and notes on progress
Develop class reading corners	PTA library furniture project Children to design class reading corner Immersion week for English – book reviews, display work for reading corners, children design reading corner	Class teacher PTA English Lead Termly	Every class to have engaging reading corner and book nooks designed by class. Children to have had input in designing of reading corner – draw what ideal place to read is. Display ideas? PTA carry out survey.	PTA to fund project! Children now need to design ideal reading corners during English lesson/Art/PPA.

Objective	Strategies	Responsible	Evaluate	Feedback and notes on progress
Adopt an author or illustrator	Authors will be adopted by classes during topics of work – classes could be named after author? Visits from authors – use Authors Abroad? Twitter/Skype to connect? Use planning/ staff meeting time to discuss DEAR opportunities	Class teacher Termly	Authors are used to link texts and extend learning. Teachers have good knowledge of books that can be used. Wide range of authors – picture books, non-fiction etc. Mindful of representation of authors/illustrators.	Author of the Term display set up.

Objective	Strategies	Responsible	Evaluate	Feedback and notes on progress
Try book making	Link to topics? Discuss progression of skills with DT lead. Book-making week? Each class makes a class book or individual books per child. Link to DT – moving picture books. Could children record audio for books and make a film of moving book?	Class teacher Art/DT Lead Yearly	Books are planned, made and evaluated by children. Linked to DT, history and geography. Shared across the school and with parents? Clear skills progression.	Year 4 have trialled with Beegu run by Steph – very successful! Discuss with KS1 lead and DT lead progression of skills.

Objective	Strategies	Responsible	Evaluate	Feedback and notes on progress
Share books	Each class needs to have a comprehensive book library with a wide range of materials available. Time during term to swap book with other children recommend etc?	Class teacher Termly	Books are rotated with library stock, supported by the school librarian. Teachers to bring a book to staff meetings to share for 5 mins at beginning?	

Objective	Strategies	Responsible	Evaluate	Feedback and notes on progress
Read widely/ Get the reading habit	Each class teacher to read with their class and demonstrate the enjoyment and appreciation of a wide range of books. Modelling of fluency and expression. Use of DEAR (Drop Everything and Read) at end of day.	Class teacher Termly	Class teachers to read for thirty minutes with their groups, so every child gets at least one read a week. Invite parents in to read to their children or in their own language. Is the school surrounded with books and words?	

Objective	Strategies	Responsible	Evaluate	Feedback and notes on progress
Keep and use books reviews	Classes to study book reviews over the course of the year's Literacy lesson. Try different types of book reviews – three-word book reviews, post-it note reviews, reviews in newspaper articles etc. how does the language and formality change?	Class teacher Termly	Children have studied and produced book reviews for a display/ class book. 'Our class is reading…' display poster on front of door. Show and Tell time for KS1 can involve reviewing and sharing books too. Are children able to review and recommend books? Can adults confident review and recommend books?	

Objective	Strategies	Responsible	Evaluate	Feedback and notes on progress
Have plenty of books around	Class libraries are plentiful and relevant to the children's learning. Books are rotated within the library's stock regularly. Use of Essex School Library boxes to replenish and rotate.	Class teacher Termly	Librarian to rotate books. Librarian and English leader to help teachers find books for topics. Is the school swimming in a range of high-quality books?	

24

Objective	Strategies	Responsible	Evaluate	Feedback and notes on progress
Perform stories	Within English and assemblies, children are given the opportunity to perform stories they have studied and incorporate drama. Staff meeting to share drama techniques beyond freeze-frame!	Class teacher Termly	Drama is effectively used to promote reading throughout curriculum. Use of ICT to evaluate performances. Invite in professional storyteller to perform? Measure impact on speaking and listening too?	

25

Objective	Strategies	Responsible	Evaluate	Feedback and notes on progress
Compete in class readathon/ competition	Class teachers to ensure that children are using the book review templates correctly. Class librarians to stick in class book review book. Book club set up by IE. Can the children beat the teachers? Can you read your height? Spellathon? etc.	Class teacher Termly	Classes are competing to read the most books. Display used to celebrate excellent reading. Buzz and excitement created around reading.	

Objective	Strategies	Responsible	Evaluate	Feedback and notes on progress
Improve home school liaison	Invite parents to come in for a presentation on reading and guided reading. Produce a booklet on tips for reading with your children. Parents invited into school to read with their children. Deliver poems and short stories to the local community? Do parents feel confident reading to and with their children?	Literacy Coordinator Yearly	Parents are used effectively to improve children's reading. Home school link is strengthened. Parents invited in to see new book corners. How effective are reading logs survey? Parent book club and book swap?	2 parent workshops run by IE on reading at bed time and questions to ask when reading – great feedback. Parents would like more time in class to read with children.

Objective	Strategies	Responsible	Evaluate	Feedback and notes on progress
Establish a swap shop for books	A swap shop enables children and parents to bring a book in and swap it for free with another book from the display. Set up in office or foyer?	Literacy Coordinator Weekly	Swap shop is introduced, promoted and checked for variety and quality. Weekly reminder on newsletter for parents? Themed book shop? E.g., poetry one half-term?	

Objective	Strategies	Responsible	Evaluate	Feedback and notes on progress
Hold events	World Book Day, Dahlicious and book themed assemblies over the course of the year. Teacher to share favourite book in assembly once a half term. Other ideas – hot chocolate Friday where children can read and drink with blankets etc, read to grandparents etc.	Literacy Coordinator Once per Term	Are events enriching the experience of reading and promoting the values we expect to see?	

Objective	Strategies	Responsible	Evaluate	Feedback and notes on progress
Create close links with booksellers	Book Fair is invited in, offering the children an opportunity to purchase books. Year 6 involved in setting up and running – application letters, posters, taking money etc.	Literacy Coordinator Yearly	Book fair is properly coordinated and evaluated for success. Where are the gaps in books – use money to close gaps.	

Objective	Strategies	Responsible	Evaluate	Feedback and notes on progress
Set up school book clubs	A weekly book club offers children and parents the chance to choose a book and be read to. Activities or just read? Trial both? Identify children to be invited to club? Train staff to run?	Literacy Coordinator Yearly	Children are encouraged to use the book club and do so enthusiastically. Book clubs are seen as special time to share joy of reading.	Have set up in own class and will submit project for Open Uni Reading for Pleasure site.

Objective	Strategies	Responsible	Evaluate	Feedback and notes on progress
Share information on local libraries	Each class is offered a chance to visit the local library over the course of the year for a tutorial session on using our local library. Library visits to link to topics for KS2? Invite librarians in to discuss their jobs? History of local library project?	Literacy Coordinator Yearly	Each class visits the library throughout year. Take part in library competitions. Library is seen as a place of wonder and joy, where children want to visit.	

Objective	Strategies	Responsible	Evaluate	Feedback and notes on progress
Train colleagues on children's literature	Authors and experts are invited in to train staff on effective practice, including use of film, whole class reading, fluency/ expression etc. Share articles, book reviews. Have a Staff Library to share books.	Literacy Coordinator Yearly	Evaluation of the training and teachers' confidence. Use of Open University Reading for Pleasure examples.	Run staff meetings on: picture books, 2 x whole class reading – monitor and observe.

Objective	Strategies	Responsible	Evaluate	Feedback and notes on progress
Collect odd, old books	Librarian to monitor the range of books used and to circulate the stock for class library. Teachers to share books they've used that may be out of the ordinary. Display photos of strange books and libraries in class/assembly?	Librarian Yearly	Class teachers to monitor. Use Twitter to widen recommendations. Can adults bring in old books from around the world? Display?	

Part 2

The 'Reader-Response' Processes

In this chapter, I am asking the question of how it is readers actually respond to books (texts). I don't think that we access this deep response through the kinds of questions that are on SATs papers and in comprehension exercises. I am offering it here as a way of thinking of response as a wide-ranging, diverse set of reactions to reading. It's for you to see how this can be adapted in your classroom and school practice in age-appropriate ways.

What does it mean to read and understand a text? The 'reader-response' processes.

I think to get a handle on this question we have to go into the processes, (the 'mind-games' if you like) that we go through as we read, and after we have read.

One way to talk about this is to call it 'comprehension' and devise a set of right/wrong answer type questions which 'prove' that we have understood a text. These often revolve round 'retrieval', 'inference', getting the 'chronology' or 'sequencing' right and so on.

The problem with this model is precisely that there are only right/ wrong answers. It treats a text as if it is an egg-box full of eggs and 'comprehension' is a matter of lifting out the eggs that are there. This is a model that refuses or rejects the idea that we 'interpret' what we read. What follows is a different model. It suggests that we take what we believe to be there (using our memories and methods of thought) reflect on it and come to conclusions or 'provisional' conclusions.

The exam-type comprehension question also refuses or rejects the extent to which in the real world the way we read is 'social'. We read, we talk, we read, we talk, we may write about what we read, we may share what we write, we talk some more, we read some more . . . and so on. Our understanding of a text, groups of texts or all reading is created and forged in social circumstances.

So, I'm posing two alternatives to 'comprehension' as it's usually understood:

a) interpretation (not 'right/wrong') and

b) social – through our interactions with each other.

As a contribution (not a final answer) to this, here is a set of processes our minds go through where we are on our own or with others as we read books. If we want to help children get an enjoyable way of reading, I suggest that at various times we need to encourage and help them develop any or all of these approaches.

Please note, these categories are not single stand-alone categories, they overlap, and they emphasise slightly different things. They are suggestions and they are for you to adapt and play with and add to.

Further – if this looks familiar it's because in my booklet *Poems and Stories for Primary and Lower Secondary Schools* I have a similar 'matrix' which was designed from a slightly different angle: a matrix for teachers to analyse their pupils' responses.

I have drawn this up partly for our students doing the MA in Children's

Literature at Goldsmiths, University of London who were interested in a matrix of response, rather than the one I have already done which is the matrix of how to analyse pupils' responses!

So here it is:

1. Experiential-relational:

When we read, we relate aspects of our own lives (and/or to the lives of people we know) to what we read. We relate what is in the text with something that has happened to me or to someone I know. One useful trigger question for this is simply to ask: 'Is there anything you've just read which reminds you of something that has happened to you, or someone you know? – can you say why? or how?' This taps into how we feel about moments in any text without asking the direct question, 'what did you feel about that?'

2. Intertextual-relational:

This is where we relate what is in the text to another text. One useful trigger for this question is: 'Is there anything you've just read which reminds you of something you've read, seen on TV, online, at the cinema, a song, a play, a show? – Why? How?' Again, this will tap into how we feel about a moment simply by tapping into another moment from another text that we feel is similar – for any reason.

3. Intratextual-relational:

This is where we relate one part of the text to another part. One useful trigger for this question arises out of a moment in a piece of literature where we ask: 'But how do we know that?' And we answer that by using something or anything that came before?' (I have a nickname for this which younger children enjoy: I call it 'harvesting' – that is, collecting up information or feelings from other parts of the text.) We harvest all the time as we read. We harvest at the same time as we predict!

4. Interrogative:

This is where we ask questions of a text and we voice puzzles and we are tentative about something. One trigger question for this is, 'Is there anything here we don't understand or are puzzled by?' This can be followed up by, 'Is there anyone here who thinks they can answer that?' And 'Does anyone have any ideas about how we can go about finding an answer to that?'

In one sense a text is a set of puzzles or we might say that the moment we start to read we are asking questions. One way to tap into this is to encourage pupils to write questions as a story or poem unfolds. Then, we might gather up these questions and see if or how we can answer them. This is a way of treating literature as a process of investigation and we as readers play the game with the writer. The writer creates situations that are inconclusive, mysterious, puzzling, intriguing and we ask the questions that the writer poses. Or we might come up with ones that the writer didn't even know they had poses. Or we might want to ask the writer a question. (Very likely) Or we might want to ask questions 'surrounding' a text e.g., are there other texts like this one? What did people think at this time (the 19th century say) about magic? Or was everyone a Christian in Tudor times? etc.

5. Semantic-significant:

This is where we have thoughts or make comments directly about what something in the text means. There are of course many traditional ways of asking questions about this. In an environment in which we are not 'telling' pupils what a text means and/or that there is only one meaning, this can be speculative and provisional before anyone reaches conclusions.

6. Structural:

This is where we indicate we are thinking about or making a comment about how a part or whole of the piece has been put together, 'constructed'. These might be thoughts about, say, why a book is in chapters, or why something happens in 'threes' in a fairy story.

Hiding behind this question is the crucial one of 'form' or 'story syntax' and the like. That is, every time we read, we are reading something that follows or uses or plays with a literary form that already exists. We have names for many of these: the 'detective novel', the 'rom-com', the 'sonnet' and so on. In terms of literary response, we will be more or less aware of these forms and these in part intermingle with our response processes. They do this through our expectations of how the 'grammar' or 'syntax' of the story or poem unfolds. Once we have read a few books which tell stories in a certain way, we start to guess what will happen, and indeed how it happens. Any book that is part of a series, becomes more or less predictable.

One feature of children's and young people's reading is how they learn these structures, plot-lines, motifs, forms and build them into their responses. We can tap into these with the 'intertextual' question above. The argument here is that reading one text is inseparable from the expectations we have based on our other readings, i.e., based on what we understand to be the 'form' of other books.

7. Selective analogising:

This where we make an analogy (or a comparison) between one part of the text and something from anywhere else (e.g., from our own experience, from another text, from something else inside the text). When we do this 'analogising' there will be an implied 'set' or 'series' being constructed by the reader around a motif or theme or feeling.

This process of analogising is extremely important even though it is often masked by seemingly trivial comments like, 'I remember a time when I was sad . . . '

The importance lies in the fact that the pupil at this point is involved in a process of creating an unstated abstraction. It is halfway (or more) towards abstract thought. Perhaps, it becomes fully abstract when the pupil(s) give that 'set' a name: e.g., 'Sadness' or 'Emotions' or some such.

I believe that it is through this process of analogising that texts give us wisdom. I cannot emphasize its importance enough.

8. Speculative:

This is where we make speculations about what might happen, what could have happened. This is any kind of thought or comment in the category of 'I wonder . . . ' or 'What if . . . ' We do this all the time as we read and we can collect these as we read.

9. Reflective:

This is where we make interpretative statements often headed by 'I think . . . ' i.e., more committed than 'speculative'. It's a considered reflection. They are more a response to the question we might ask of ourselves like, 'so what do we think of that moment/character/ scene/landscape/cityscape etc?'

10. Narratological:

This is where we have thoughts or make comments about how the story or poem has been told e.g., about narrators, methods of unfolding a story, what is held back, what is revealed (the mechanism of 'reveal-conceal') , how we know what someone in the story or poem thinks, how we think or describe the fact that we go forwards and backwards in time in a story. (This is a whole subject in itself: 'Narratology'.) It may include an awareness of how stories have episodes, or sudden 'turns' or 'red herrings', flashbacks, flash-forwards etc.

11. Evaluative:

This is where we make value judgements (in our minds or in talk with others) about aspects of a text as a whole. These can be comments about 'significance', 'what the author is getting at . . . ', or 'why someone in the text said 'x''. Or even, what the 'message' is or 'what this is about' or what this story 'is trying to say'. They may well also be moral judgements about fair/unfair; good/bad etc. Evaluative, in other words, can be these moments during a story or after where we make value-judgements.

12. Eureka moments:

This is where we announce that we have suddenly 'got it' – an experience that many of us have when we think we know 'who's done it' or 'why someone has done it'.

13. Effects:

This is where we sense that an 'effect' has been created in us (or in others we have observed) because of the way something has been written. 'This made me jump . . . ' 'This made me sad . . . ' Response journals, or post-it notes on poem-posters and the like can 'grab' these very well. This can be a way of tracing what has been called the 'affect' – firstly how we are 'affected' by a text (did it make me sad? happy? afraid? tense? full of hope? full of dread? why?) or looking to see what aspects of the text seemed to create that way in which I was affected?

14. Storying:

This is where we make a comment which is in essence another story. This is not trivial. As with 'analogising' (above) it will almost certainly involve the making of a 'set' or a 'series' i.e., something has been selected from the original text in order to trigger off the new one.

This is an implied generalisation or abstraction. From a teaching point of view, this is one way 'in' to enabling pupils to begin to articulate abstract ideas about a text.

15. Descriptive:

This is where we recount aspects of the text. We might do this in our day-dreaming as we read, after we have read, or in talk with others later. This may well be more significant than it first appears because (as teachers) we can ask, why was this moment selected for the recount? (i.e., 'Why do you think you've described that bit of the story?') Again, this may well be part of 'analogising' and/or 'storying'.

16. Grammatical:

This is where we find our attention drawn to the structure of sentences – syntax, or how individual words are used grammatically. There are of course many right/wrong ways of asking questions about this. We might begin by asking questions about this by asking pupils to explore and investigate along the lines of e.g., finding similar or contrasting ways in which sentences are constructed . . . and asking why would that be? What is achieved by doing that? An author like Dickens varies his sentence structures enormously: one moment very long, many clause sentences: the next, rapid-fire, short sharp repetitive structures.

One way to 'discover' this is through reading or performing out loud. There are ways of drawing attention to the word-classes (nouns, adjectives, adverbs, verbs). Again, ideally this can be investigative first and be provisional: why do we think a writer has used this or that word-class? Ideally, there won't be one answer to the question!

Traditional grammar tends to use ways of describing e.g., sentence types as the main or sole way of doing something e.g., 'commands'. In fact, if we use a word like 'command' or 'the future' or many other of these terms, we can see when we look at real texts that we have many different ways of e.g., commanding, or expressing 'the future'.

If we ask of e.g., someone bossy in a text, 'how do we know he's bossy?' we may well find that it's because he has been created as using a variety of ways of commanding people, not just the one. In other words grammar makes 'sense' in many ways. It's the tools we use to convey meaning and we have many different tools to do similar things, as with creating a character who is bossy, who might deliver orders 'Do this!' or use another grammar and say, 'I want you all to . . . ' Or, 'All children must . . . ' They are all 'bossy' ways of going on, using different aspects of grammar.

We might find that the way into grammar is via different and differing 'clusters' of intention and meaning.

17. Prosodic:

This is where we notice or we draw attention to the sound of parts of the whole of a piece i.e., the 'music' of it. I have outlined in my book *What is Poetry?* (Walker) how you can invite pupils to determine this themselves by using what I call 'secret strings' i.e., finding links between parts of poems whether linked by sound or by meaning. These secret strings are the links between repeated sounds of letters, words, rhythms or the repeated or patterned way in which writers use images (similar or contrasted) . . . or indeed any links we might find or make. If we think it or say it and can prove it, it's a link! Much of this is on the edge of our consciousness as we read because writers try to conceal it. Writers try to make links that are there but affect us without words in the text saying that that is what they want to do. This is a crucial part of how literature is as much about feeling as it is about ideas. A key way in which writers create feeling is through 'secret strings' . . . repeated sounds, images, and motifs.

These links are in fact different and differing kinds of 'cohesion'. Sometimes these are grammatical – as with first using someone's name and then using a pronoun ('Michael' and then 'he'), or they might be at the level of sound or image.

(Note in passing: You can argue that what defines literature is that it is a specialised form of cohesion!)

18. Effect of interactions:

This is where we notice or we draw attention to how people interact i.e., how people (any character) treats another, how they 'relate' and what is the outcome of how they relate. In my experience, this is more valuable than simply trying to describe 'character'. If we think of scenes or moments in literature, they end. We can think of these as 'outcomes'. A writer like Enid Blyton traditionally tells her readers what this outcome is: 'That served her right.' It is one of the marked difference between writing for young readers and older ones that these 'outcomes' are often more marked in books for younger readers. Even so, all texts leave 'gaps' in which these outcomes or effects of the outcomes are there for us to wonder about and speculate about. We 'dive in' to these 'gaps' and come to conclusions or mini-conclusions.

19. Imaginative-re-interpretive:

This is where we move to another artistic medium (film, photography, drawing, painting, model-making, pottery, dance, music, drama, making power-points, sound-tracks, etc) in order to interpret what we have been reading or viewing . . . this may well involve more 'generalising' or 'abstract thought' than first appears, because it involves us in 'selecting' something from the original text and creating some kind of 'set' or 'series' with this as and when we create something new. If pupils are asked 'why' this can be teased out.

(Passing note: this used to be thought of as one of the highest-status activities on the block. When we visit great mansions and stately homes, the ceilings and walls are often covered with paintings and murals of re-interpretations of classical literature. At some point in our idea of 'education' we downgraded 're-interpretation' as some kind of 'artsy' thing that is 'kinda nice for those that want to do it' rather than a profound way in which we can explore the ideas and feelings in a moment of a text or the whole text.)

20. Emotional flow – or the 'affect':

These are the thoughts and comments which show how our feelings towards the protagonists change. Some people have invented 'flow maps' where you can draw up a kind of graph or chart, with the key moments in the plot along the bottom axis, and emotional states on the vertical axis . . . then you can label the line on the graph. This might be a graph say in which I felt more or less hostile to someone, or I was more or less amused by this or that chapter. You can create graphs where you have several lines, with each line representing a different emotion: fear, humour, tension, mystery. Then as the story proceeds, you make your line go up or down across the graph.

This is one of the key dynamics of a text. This is what writers spend hours trying to create. Writers are interested in trying to win a reader's sympathy for one character, the dislike of another. They may well want to play tricks and first win the sympathy and then 'disappoint' by making that character behave 'badly'. There are many variations to this 'flow' that the reader experiences and that the reader makes meanings, and comes to conclusions and value-judgements about whether things are right or wrong, fair or unfair, good or bad, nice or nasty, and so on.

But it's not just about 'character'. It's about the sensation of the moment or scene we are watching.

When we set up 'charts' we describe this flow. And from these charts we can go back into the text to find why or how we think the writer helped create this. Or we might ask of ourselves, why did I feel that annoyance with that character at that moment? What is it about me that thinks that kind of behaviour is arrogant etc.

Once again, there is an interaction between what we think is in the text and what it is about me that came to have that feeling?

We might ask of ourselves or discuss, which was the most important 'moment' when our emotions or feelings were flowing?

21. 'Author intention':

This might come partly under the category of 'speculative' – above – i.e., what the author could have written, might not have written, might have written in another way, or ultimately why do we think the author wrote it this way.

Or it might be part of 'effect' i.e., how has the author created an effect. Word of warning: if this is separated from 'how it affected me' or 'how it affected someone else', this is of course speculation.

The routine of a good deal of 'criticism' is to assume precisely the opposite i.e., because there is a certain literary feature – e.g., alliteration using a 'hard' sound, that it has a specific 'effect' – e.g., being insistent or heavy – and that the author intended these, which may or may not be the case. A huge amount of school-based criticism comes from this dubious premise: a specific literary feature has a specific effect. This can easily become formulaic and if it doesn't overlap in any way with the pupils' or readers' experience then it's just gobbledegook learned for exams.

We might encourage speculation about author-intention by simply asking pupils, would you like to ask the author any questions? Then we might ask one pupil to be that author and the rest of us interview the 'author'. Whenever the pupil can't answer the question, we might ask ourselves how can we find out more in order to answer it? A book? The internet?

22. Contextual:

Every piece of literature comes from a time and place. The person reading or spectating it will not be in exactly the same time and place as the author. Many responses and critical ideas and thoughts go on because of this 'gap'. Students may well know or speculate about the gap, or the context ('They didn't used to do that sort of thing in those days') and of course, may ask questions and/or we offer them information or they are encouraged to research the context(s).

Between us we have very different awarenesses of contexts of a piece of writing. Give me an ancient Chinese text and I know very little. Give me a text written about London last year, I have a lot. Even so, for all of us there is always some context we know, some we think we know and we bring this contextual knowledge to a text.

We can of course find out much more and traditionally, texts by e.g., Shakespeare, have a whole apparatus of 'context' around them that students are given. There are varying degrees to which this affects our response processes. Some of it may be so academic or distant that it has little. Some may be very directly affecting.

I have found in ideal situations the most affecting contextual knowledge starts out by coming from the pupils' first questions about a text or about an author. They are those puzzles and queries which hang in the air around a text.

We can draw these out, encourage the process of asking the questions and do what we can to set up the means of finding out. 'Is Roald Dahl still alive?' etc.

23. Representational or symbolic:

This is where we have thoughts or make comments about what we think something 'represents'. This might be about 'character' where we say that a person 'represents' the class or type he or she comes from . . . 'she's a typical x kind of person'. It might be about parts of the landscape or the nature of the landscape – as it represents a particular kind of challenge to the protagonist. It could be a feature in the landscape/cityscape i.e., a particular kind of tree or building. It could be a single object that represents something more than itself – a torn piece of paper. And so on.

People often say to me that *We're Going on a Bear Hunt* is a 'bit like life' – you can't go over it, you can't go under it, you have to go through it. That's a representational thought and comment.

24. Extra-textual:

These are thoughts or comments that have apparently nothing to do with what's in the text and are about what's going on in the classroom or they are about pupils' interactions. Often these are as they seem to be but just occasionally they may well relate to how the pupils are interpreting e.g., a personal comment about 'You always say things like that . . .' may well be an indirect comment about this text and others.

25. Causational:

These are the thoughts or moments when we say or think that something happened or someone thought 'x' because . . . Anytime we say to ourselves . . . 'Oh, that's why she . . .' These moments of realisation of cause (or imagined cause) are crucial to how and why we read. Part (as very important part) of the human mind hunts for explanations and reasons. We are drawn to wanting to know people's motives and the outcomes of those motives. This is at the heart of fiction and narratives of many kinds – perhaps of life too.

We ask ourselves questions like, 'why did he do that?' all the time.

So, just as important as the conclusion in this matter ('that's why he did it') is the speculation about 'why he did it'.

In terms of teaching, I think it's vital to not state a reason before the pupils' own speculations. It's crucial to leave the 'why' speculations hanging in the air for as long as possible before finding out and coming to some kind of conclusion as to why. Speculation is reading!

26. What else?

What other processes – stand-alone or overlapping with any of the above, would you put into this matrix of response?

Final note: there is a reading-list which informs all of the above. I will provide that at the end of this book.

Part 3

'Things I Believe Help Children Become *Readers*'

This list comes from classroom teacher David Keyte from Yattendon School.

Things I believe help children become 'readers':

1. Lots of excited adult talk about books.

2. Regularly share blurbs and extracts of books.

3. Comfy reading.

4. Time for class books every day.

5. Time for independent reading every day.

6. Make authors 'real' through Twitter interactions etc.

7. Make reading 'cool' (pictures of celebrities reading etc.)

8. Use recently released books in reading/guided reading lessons.

9. Create opportunities for children to share what they are reading with their classmates.

10. Never dissuade children from trying out a book they like the look of.

11. Walk around school with a book.

12. Regularly ask children 'What are you reading?' when walking around school.

13. Create an excitement around your own book shelf at home.

14. Talk about the aesthetics of books.

15. Create bookmarks with your class.

Part 4

How Does Reveal-Conceal Work? How do Writers do it? Why is it Important?

In this chapter I am looking at what I think is one of the most important techniques that writers use to keep us reading. It's known as 'Reveal-Conceal'.

This is the opening of Shakespeare's play *Hamlet*. If you are reading this with some other people, you could read it as if you were doing a radio play!

ACT I

SCENE I. Elsinore. A platform before the castle.

FRANCISCO at his post. Enter to him BERNARDO

I. BERNARDO
Who's there?

2. FRANCISCO
Nay, answer me: stand, and unfold yourself.

3. BERNARDO
Long live the king!

4. FRANCISCO
Bernardo?

5. BERNARDO
He.

6. FRANCISCO
You come most carefully upon your hour.

7. BERNARDO
'Tis now struck twelve; get thee to bed, Francisco.

8. FRANCISCO
For this relief much thanks: 'tis bitter cold,
And I am sick at heart.

9. BERNARDO
Have you had quiet guard?

10. FRANCISCO
Not a mouse stirring.

11. BERNARDO
Well, good night.
If you do meet Horatio and Marcellus,
The rivals of my watch, bid them make haste.

12. FRANCISCO
I think I hear them. Stand, ho! Who's there?

Enter HORATIO and MARCELLUS

13. HORATIO
Friends to this ground.

14. MARCELLUS
And liegemen to the Dane.

15. FRANCISCO
Give you good night.

16. MARCELLUS
O, farewell, honest soldier:
Who hath relieved you?

17. FRANCISCO
Bernardo has my place.
Give you good night.

Exit

18. MARCELLUS
Holla! Bernardo!

19. BERNARDO
Say,
What, is Horatio there?

20. HORATIO
A piece of him.

21. BERNARDO
Welcome, Horatio: welcome, good Marcellus.

22. MARCELLUS
What, has this thing appear'd again to-night?

23. BERNARDO
I have seen nothing.

24. MARCELLUS
Horatio says 'tis but our fantasy,
And will not let belief take hold of him
Touching this dreaded sight, twice seen of us:
Therefore I have entreated him along
With us to watch the minutes of this night;
That if again this apparition come,
He may approve our eyes and speak to it.

25. HORATIO
Tush, tush, 'twill not appear.

26. BERNARDO
Sit down awhile;
And let us once again assail your ears,
That are so fortified against our story
What we have two nights seen.

27. HORATIO
Well, sit we down,
And let us hear Bernardo speak of this.

28. BERNARDO
Last night of all,
When yond same star that's westward from the pole
Had made his course to illume that part of heaven
Where now it burns, Marcellus and myself,
The bell then beating one—

Enter Ghost

So here are 28 little speeches that happen before we read in the stage directions: 'Enter Ghost'. If, we put ourselves in the shoes of the writer, William Shakespeare, and we have a story to tell, it's clear that he has made some choices here about how to do it. For example, he could have begun this play with 'Enter Ghost'. He could have begun with what is the next line after 'Enter Ghost' which is: 'Peace, break thee off: look where it comes again!' (spoken by Marcellus). Shakespeare could, perhaps, have got all four men to come on to the stage talking about this ghost that they've seen before and then to be suddenly confronted with it again. It's easy to think of different ways this scene could begin.

This leads me to ask, why do it this way?

Line 1 is a classic example of how writers do 'reveal-conceal'. We pretend that we are revealing a new piece of information whilst at the same time, concealing or withholding another. A character asking a question that he or she doesn't the know the answer of, is one way to do it. If the reader doesn't know the answer – as with this example – then the question is both a question and a cunning way to get the audience to wonder along with the person asking the question. 'Who's there?' says Bernardo. Yes, who? we ask.

As this is a play and not a story, we don't know exactly how Bernardo says this but we can figure out from how fearful they are later in the scene that a good way to perform this line is to be absolutely terrified. This will add to the 'conceal' element in the question. (Think of the alternatives, e.g., Bernardo is drunk and he calls out, 'who's there?' as if he's hoping for a bit of company.) Making Bernardo fearful will build up our expectations and fears and – key word for 'reveal-conceal': dread. A lot of fiction works on the basis that we readers and audience fear or dread a bad or awful outcome. We may have this dread confirmed or relieved, depending on what kind of story it is.

So, the reveal is a guard. The conceal is something along the lines of, who does this guard dread? Who is he afraid of?

It's a great start to a story.

Line 2 from Francisco confirms the dread. It is in a way an echo of what Bernardo has just said. They are equally full of dread. Line 3 is in effect the password that informs the other party that neither is a threat to another. In effect the withholding of what or who it is they dread is being postponed while we have a second of relief along with the two men that the object of their dread hasn't turned up. But what is the object of their dread? Still withheld.

Line 7 tells us that this is the changing of the guard – more reveal than conceal. So far so good.

Line 8 stokes the dread: Francisco has 'much relief' – a grim Shakespearean pun. 'Relief' from what? Why? That's more conceal at work there. We are given the atmospherics of the fact that it's cold – that's reveal rather than conceal.

Line 9 is another example of the questioning method of reveal-conceal. We are invited to wonder. Our questioning is informed by the fear that we saw and heard when Bernardo and Francisco first met. A bit more conceal being stoked here.

Line 10 reassures the guards. We are perhaps reassured too but now we are into another form of 'conceal' – the delay. We know in our bones that something is afoot but we are being told that nothing is happening. (Dramatic irony).

Line 21 brings in Horatio and Marcellus – more reveal than conceal. But the next line . . .

Line 22 we have the question method yet again. This is building up a sense that this group of people really don't know what's going on or perhaps more particularly why the thing that is happening keeps happening.

Speech 24 is interesting from the reveal-conceal perspective: first we have the word 'fantasy' and then a bit later the word 'dreaded'. Fantasy raises the question of whether they are imagining things. 'Dreaded' chimes with the characters and our sense of foreboding. It stokes the dread – of course. It works as 'what the characters dread so the audience dreads'.

Then we have the word 'apparition'. This is a great reveal. We now know what it is that the characters dread but it is sufficiently vague and full of unknown potential to keep the conceal going. An apparition of what? Of who? And why is it here? Lots of conceal in and amongst the reveal.

Speeches 25 and 26 show us that Horatio is the reassuring voice, possibly the more rational voice amongst them. This serves the function of revealing Horatio to us, who will of course later be Hamlet's reassuring and loyal friend. But he also can act in this moment as an echo to our own rational thoughts; e.g., that we might not believe in apparitions. Hiding behind that, though, is the conceal of: 'Well if an apparition does appear, that will outweigh a rationalist's suspicions'. (It's a technique often used on TV shows about ghosts or hypnotism: win over the most rational person in the room!)

Speeches 25-28 are 'delay' methods of reveal-conceal. Notice that Bernardo in 28 has gone into Classical mode of speech, lines that tell us of settings, visuals, states of the weather and the like. We might well feel at this point: 'Get on with it!' but it's being withheld (concealed), right up to the moment that the Ghost appears and is revealed.

Our sense of anticipation, tension, foreboding and dread should be pretty well stoked up for this moment.

This opening is a good example of how writers do reveal-conceal.

I'm interested in why it is that a process that I think is central to how writers write, how and why readers read (excitement, tension, foreboding, confirmation of one's fears or contradiction of them with reassurance) is hardly touched on in the usual school-based criticism.

I've identified several aspects of reveal-conceal here: e.g., questioning, delay, minor reassurance en route to the object of our dread, stoking fears through use of words like 'dread', talking of an object of our dread in vague terms – like 'apparition' and so on.

We could call this the beginning of a 'grammar' of reveal-conceal.

In classes, you might want to do 'reveal-conceal' spotting! How does a writer, appear to tell us something but at the same time, not tell us? So, as one very simple example, if a story begins, 'Once upon a winter night . . . ' this reveals that it is 'night' but the 'once' tells us that something is coming and this, for the moment, is 'concealed'. If, as in *Where the Wild Things Are* the narrative says, that Max 'wanted to be where someone loved him best of all', this tells us what he wants (reveal) but the 'someone' doesn't tell us who! Who is this 'someone'? This is the 'gap' that is left by 'reveal-conceal'.

What you can do with a class is: 'look for gaps'. You can ask them children/students to be detectives, looking for 'gaps' and asking them how will they 'fill' them. This is actually an important theoretical idea to do with 'interpretation', made age-appropriate by this device of 'looking for gaps' and asking 'how to fill them'.

Part 5

SPaG 2018 Analysed Question by Question. What's Wrong With it?

In this chapter I am looking for what I think is the opposite of a good way to interpret texts. That's because I believe that the SPaG/GPS type questions are not about real language-in-use. They are about examples of language invented with the sole purpose of illustrating what is actually and only 'sentence grammar'. Language-in-use is always more than this. It is created for social purposes (our interactions or social life, if you like) and any 'bit' or 'chunk' that we look at, will always be linked to language-in-use that comes before it and after it. The links will be to do with this social purpose but also with the history of what kind of conversation or type of text this is – what we call its 'genre'. We always use language within patterns and types of language.

It's possible to treat language-in-use as a fascinating territory to explore – just as we might explore a beach or a department store. We can investigate these things in order to spot patterns, types and repeated motifs. This gives us knowledge about language-in-use across a wider spectrum of use than 'the sentence'.

SPaG 2018 – Question by Question

Here are some detailed comments on the 2018 SPaG paper. The

reason why I've done this is because I think that we should take on the arguments that lie behind this test. One way is to talk about the politics that brought it in (as with the Bew Report on Assessment and Accountability being hijacked by Michael Gove so that he could a) pursue his pet agenda of 'grammar' and b) to create a means of measuring teachers' 'performance' (their 'input') by testing children's 'performance' (their 'output'). This is a mechanical and mechanistic idea of what is a performance or 'activity' in a classroom. It is reducing the activity to the teaching of right/wrong answers. It also reduces children to being what scientists call a 'black box' – that is treating the process (in this case the child, the child's thinking and the child's learning) as irrelevant, because input is being tested on the basis of output. This tells us very little about what really matters – how children think and learn.

Anyway, here are the questions:

Question 1

Insert a comma in the correct place in the sentence below.

'Although he was the youngest Tom was one of the tallest.'

As a general comment, it's important to point out that the sentences used for this test are ones made up by the examiners. They are contrived in order to illustrate the point that they want to demonstrate and they have no context around them. The 'sentence' (as defined by the gov.uk 'Glossary' and by the test itself) is a bizarre, context-free spurt of language.

'A sentence is a group of words which are grammatically connected to each other but not to any words outside the sentence.'

These sentences are examples of pointless, unrealistic utterances. Surely, we want children to acquire a knowledge about language which is linked directly to how it is used in its many different ways. We use language in order to make meanings. These people, (who regard themselves as experts in language) have missed this key point about language. It's no surprise though, because their model of 'grammar' is an attempt to devise rules about sentences and language without reference to meaning, without reference to social purpose, and without reference to why people choose to say or write things in the way that they do. Or, they think that the reason why people say or write something is because of the 'rules' embedded in the 'sentences'. This cuts out the idea that people have invented language and use language and change language in order to create meaning in many different and varied ways. It's not language which determines how and why we use language but it is people (us) who choose to use language in certain ways.

Question 8

Which sentence is grammatically correct?

Tomorrow we went shopping at the sales.
In three weeks' time, I will be on holiday.
Next weekend, we had gone to the river to fish.
Last summer, we swim at the beach and collect seashells.

This is an example of where their use of the word 'grammar' (or 'grammatically' etc.) strays into meaning. Another way to put this question is to ask something like, 'Three of these questions don't really make sense. One of them does. Which one?', but because the examiners' definition of 'grammar' is slippery and inconsistent (one moment using it to mean something defined by 'structure' as with Question 1, the next – as with this question – using it to include meaning. That is, the only way to get this question right is from the meaning of the words and phrases of the sentences. To spell it out: it's only by knowing the meaning of the word 'Tomorrow' and the phrase 'we went' that we know that the sentence is 'wrong' (i.e., doesn't make sense).

Question 9

Which verb is the synonym of the verb produce?

make
buy
sell
trade

Just to be clear: 'synonyms' and 'antonyms' are nothing to do with 'grammar'. They are some weird vestige left over from ancient rhetoric and public school education. They have no real linguistic value. In reality, synonyms and antonyms don't exist. That's to say, one of the whole points about the language we use is that we know that no one word means exactly the same as another. No one word is some kind of exact opposite of another. It is misleading to tell children that this is how we make language work. In fact, when we speak and write, we do other things with similar or un-similar words, like e.g., use words to 'clarify' or 'illustrate' or 'match' or 'add nuance' or 'contrast' or 'compare'. Rather than waste time teaching children that such non-existent things exist, we can easily invite them to find similarities, differences and contrasts and ask them to wonder why writers and speakers might want to do such things. Such things are embedded in the most basic of stories that the children know, fairy tales like *Cinderella* with their stark similarities and contrasts between people or between the 'then' and 'now' of the story. We can reach this by thinking of language as something we can explore.

Question 10

Which sentence is a command?
You should bring a coat.
You will need a coat in case it rains.
I am going to bring a coat.
Bring a coat in case it rains.

This is an example of where the examiners are hoist on their own petard. The categories of sentence that they've come up with: 'Question', 'Statement', 'Command' and 'Exclamation' were originally devised on the basis of the 'verb forms' and/or 'verb structures' within them. So we have ways of being 'interrogative' in English e.g., by writing such things as 'Are you . . . ?' Or, 'Is the car . . . ?' Again, our ways of making a 'statement' can be 'You are . . . ' or 'The car is . . . '. Commands traditionally were defined by such verb forms as 'Go!' or 'Keep left' (known as the imperative) and exclamations were (in theory!) limited to sentences that began with such words as 'How . . . and 'What . . . ' while at the same time not being used to ask questions! (Difficult to follow? Sorry, I didn't make this stuff up.)

Anyway, the point is that these sentence-types were devised on the basis of grammar and language structure. This was 'pure' grammar, in that sense. They also had supposedly difficult or off-putting words like 'indicative' or 'imperative'. Clearly, these examiners decided that they were too hard for 10 and 11 year olds (probably true) so they came up with what they thought were more user-friendly terms like 'question' and 'command'. Now here's the problem they've given themselves: you can only deduce such things from the meaning. But this gives them the problem of saying that such-and-such a sentence is a 'command' and another one is not – based on meaning alone. Go back to the question. The sentence: 'You should bring a coat' can be – purely on the basis of the meaning of the words – be a 'command' in the everyday sense. Imagine a teacher: 'Children: you should bring your coats!' In fact, by their own definition of a command, even 'You must bring your coats' wouldn't be a 'command'! Clearly, we use a word like 'command' in real life (as opposed to the *Alice in Wonderland* world of 'grammar') to mean 'to command' and we can choose a variety of structures to do this depending on who it is who's speaking and who that speaker is speaking to. A word like 'command' has been plucked from real life and applied in one very specific way.

The end result of all this is that the question is not valid. If one of the choices in a multiple-choice question is reasonable and feasible but is 'wrong' then the test fails. In this case, it fails because they've fudged their own 'grammar' (supposedly based on 'word-class, structure, grammar and function').

Question 12

Which option completes the sentence in the past perfect?

As a piece of rubric this is really quite annoying. The word 'option' and the phrase 'completes the sentence in the past perfect' is jargon. If you really wanted to find out if children could recognise this way of talking about the past, you could phrase the sentence in a much more helpful way. You could say e.g., 'Choose from the four examples, the past perfect and write it into the sentence so that the sentence makes sense.'

Incidentally, this term 'past perfect' is a lovely example of grammar diarrhoea. Every few years, they come up with new terms for the same old, same old! For decades this form of the verb was called the 'pluperfect'. That's how I learned it when I did English, French and German at school. We had the 'perfect' (which is one way we can express something in the past) and then the 'pluperfect' which to my ears at least made it sound 'even more in the past' as if it was 'perfect-plus'. Now there is this newer term 'past perfect' which is really very hard for a 10/11 year old to squeeze into something that gives them a clue as to why e.g., 'I had set' should be called 'past perfect'! What is 'past perfect' about 'I had set'? I dunno. Presumably, if some people earned a living for a week by coming up this new name, they must think it is in some deep way an improvement. It's not.

Question 13

Which sentence is written in Standard English?

Two sports teams come to our school yesterday.

My friend was tidying the classroom.
Today the children done their school play.
The teachers was going to send a letter next week.

We can ask of this question, 'What is Standard English'? In order to be able to answer the question, the children would need to know the Standard English forms of subject-verb formations using the verbs 'to come', 'to be', 'to do' and 'to go'. This invites a particular kind of teaching – much loved by these grammarians, though they sometimes deny it – doing 'conjugations'. As a grammar school pupil (N.B. NOT at primary school) we chanted conjugations of verbs in French, German and Latin lessons. It was reckoned, even by the most formal of teachers, that we didn't need to do it in English. Do these examiners think it's a good idea for us to do it in English? Where's the theory or research showing this?

The easiest and most fun way to explore Standard English and non-Standard verb forms is to use a piece of fiction where the narration is in Standard and the dialogue is in non-Standard. The most obvious of these is passages in Dickens. I would love to think that it is possible for teachers to find time (in an overloaded curriculum) to approach this question in this way: using a passage of real writing for a purpose (like Dickens, or a modern author for children) and exploring their use of Standard and non-Standard. This can then be used to compare and contrast it with the use of English by people they know or see on TV. By the way – open question: is there a good and useful text-book that teachers are using which lays out interesting and fun ways in which the differences between Standard and non-Standard can be taught?

Question 14

Tick the sentence that uses a dash correctly.

Call me pedantic but in actual fact 'sentences' don't 'use' anything.

Sentences are made up by human beings and it's us who 'use' dashes, not sentences. I regard this as methodological madness. We keep turning language and parts of language into living beings which can 'do' things. This takes away from the fact that we use language to do things that we want it to do. We make choices with language. We make meaning with language. We do this for reasons – which are very interesting to figure out and speculate about. If we get into a mindset that it's the 'sentence' that 'uses' the dash 'correctly', it invites us to think that there is some mysterious power that rules over us, embedded in something like a 'sentence' which has the power of telling us how to use a dash. No, we choose how to use dashes and the world of dashes is a very wobbly, irregular world. As it happens the 'wrong' answers are so wrong in this question, that how the examiners have used the dash 'correctly' is clear. Even so, the idea that there are only a few 'correct' ways to use a dash is dubious. A train journey in the London Underground looking at posters and ads, or indeed two minutes looking at the poetry of Emily Dickinson, or the writing of Lewis Carroll and you'll find dashes being used in all sorts of exciting and odd ways.

If these examiners want children to have 'knowledge about language' and want them to see the wonderful ways in which we can use language, then the way to do it is not through telling them there are 'correct' ways to use dashes but rather to investigate some ways in which writers have used dashes and are coming up with new good ways for themselves.

Question 16

Which sentence must not end with an exclamation mark?

What a hilarious film that was
I loved the opening scene
Was the ending funny
I have never laughed so much

The sub-text here is quite funny. The Schools Minister, Nick Gibb, tied himself in knots trying to explain the proper way to use exclamation marks. Someone pushed him into the spotlight to 'explain' that this new 'grammar' stuff was defining what an 'exclamation' is and that these needed an exclamation mark. I think SPaG has retreated from this – unworkable even by their own standards – and here they are being all 'liberal' by suggesting that it's OK to use exclamation marks on sentences that are not exclamations. Phew! (See what I did there?) But yet again, this has given them another problem: actually you can bung exclamation marks wherever you want. The sentence 'Was the ending funny' is of course the usual way in which we ask questions so in their world, you 'can't' have an exclamation mark at the end. But these are sentences taken out of context. In fact, if you have the intonation of someone of e.g., a Jewish background – like me! – or someone fond of a particular kind of ironic use of language then we use a structure like this to indeed make exclamations and not ask questions. Older readers will remember the late England football manager, Graham Taylor, saying, 'Do I not like that' (in reference to the fact that Holland were beating England). It was not a question. It was an exclamation. When put into writing, it would be perfectly OK to put an exclamation mark. In fact, I can hear people like my father or grandfather saying, 'Was the ending funny!' by way of saying it wasn't funny. Giving children sentences taken out of context demonstrates above all else that the supposed 'real' meaning or use that the examiners have in mind is not a universal meaning or use. They don't seem to realise this.

Another useless question from the examiners, and one which hasn't taken notice of how people are using language in real life.

Questions 18, 20, 21, 22, 23, 24
(and many others in this exam)

These all ask of the children to get the names of 'word-classes' correct. We should remember here that there have been times when those in control of this stuff have said that they didn't want to go back to the days of 'parsing'. This was an ancient exercise of taking sentences and calling out the word-classes and 'cases' etc. of the words in the sentences. Teachers would walk round a class barking out one of the words in a piece of Latin and you had to bark back that it was, say, the 'accusative case of 'puella'' or some such. Really! I am not making this up.

It was felt, even by the types of people who set these tests, that this was of limited use, and might actually be counter-productive in keeping children's interest in language alive. In fact, it's very hard to learn how to do such questions, asked in such decontextualised ways, without having to do some form of parsing.

To be fair (why should I be?!) there are ways of doing a limited form of this in fun ways that appeal to children's interest in 'spotting' and 'collecting' things. We can indeed spend short periods of time, saying, 'Let's spot the adverbs in this set of instructions' or such like. It is one way to get to know and remember some of the terms.

By the way, Question 24 asks the children to use pronouns 'correctly'. Interestingly, this use is across three sentences. In the government's own glossary here again is the definition of a 'sentence':

> 'A sentence is a group of words which are grammatically connected to each other but not to any words outside the sentence.'

In fact, this question proves that this statement from the glossary is nonsense. We often use pronouns to refer back from one sentence to another. We say – as here – 'Jack' – in one sentence and in the next we say, 'he'. This grammar even has a word for doing this: 'cohesion'. It's about the only word they've borrowed from the great linguist M.A.K. Halliday who spent a lifetime trying to incorporate use, purpose, function, meaning and choice into grammar, something that these people setting these questions seem resolutely to ignore. You

can navigate yourself to some of these other ways of talking about language and grammar here:
www.en.wikipedia.org/wiki/Functional_theories_of_grammar

Question 25

Which sentence is the most formal?

Watching too much television should be avoided.
You shouldn't watch too much TV.
Watching too much TV isn't a good idea.
You really should try not watch loads of telly.

I put out a question about this on Twitter and Facebook: where are the text books which give teachers and pupils some kind of definition and a grid of what is 'formal' English? There's no definition of it on the government's own glossary, which boasts in its first sentence:

'The following glossary includes all the technical grammatical terms used in the programmes of study for English, as well as others that might be useful.'

The only place it's used is in this passage:

'Some people use Standard English all the time, in all situations from the most casual to the most formal, so it covers most registers. The aim of the national curriculum is that everyone should be able to use Standard English as needed in writing and in relatively formal speaking.'

No definitions are given here of 'casual', and 'formal'. They aren't grammatical terms anyway. They are terms to do with etiquette and one person's 'formal' is another person's 'casual'. There is also that old familiar slide going on here in which 'Standard English' is used here as a term to include 'spoken English'.

The old agreement between linguists is that we don't speak Standard English — we write it. That's because when we speak, we repeat ourselves, we self-correct, we insert many ums and ers and 'y'knows', we often don't finish what we're saying so the sentences are 'incomplete' and so on. In speaking we tend to avoid too many conditions on the main thing we want to say (i.e., not too many of 'if', 'when' 'although' type clauses. The only time we speak Standard English is when we read a speech or recite something written.

Clearly, here the claim is being made that we do speak Standard English and it's something to do with 'formal' situations. But in fact, if Standard English is being nudged into how we speak, then it's quite easy to use non-Standard forms when we are in formal situations. Alan Sugar does it quite often in 'The Apprentice'!

The point is that some people use mostly 'standard forms' when they speak. Some people mostly use non-standard forms. Some people hop between both. Some people hardly ever do. Children who hardly ever use the standard forms for, let's say, the use of the verb 'to be' (e.g., 'we was' etc.) have to learn the Standard 'we were' in order to pass this exam. Some will say that they have to learn it in order to have an equal chance to go for jobs.

However, that said, it isn't the Standard English question being asked here. It's the one about 'formal'. Perhaps, I thought, the answer to this problem is in the glossary's definition of 'register':

> 'Classroom lessons, football commentaries and novels use different registers of the same language, recognised by differences of vocabulary and grammar. Registers are 'varieties' of a language which are each tied to a range of uses, in contrast with dialects, which are tied to groups of users.'

Is this trying to say (1) that there is one register in a 'classroom lesson' and another in a football commentary? It's ambiguous! (What?

Grammarians writing ambiguously? Surely not.) It could mean (2) that lessons, commentaries and novels use different registers within them. The first meaning (1) is false. The second one (2) is right. Either way, I don't think it's much use if we want to know what a 'register' is. That's because 'register' is a fuzzy quasi-literary category often used by critics when they (we!) recognise people in life or in texts switching from one use of language to another, according to where that kind of language is usually used. Famous examples: Margaret Thatcher using the word 'frit'; Ronald Reagan using the expression, 'You ain't seen nothing yet'.

I'm afraid that saying this is 'in contrast' to use of dialect, is palpably wrong. One way we switch registers is to go from e.g., Standard English forms to non-standard ones, otherwise known as switching between 'dialects'. We do that for many interesting reasons.

Meanwhile, back with 'formal', I have no idea how the children can be expected to get this except through some kind of hunch. I wonder how teachers are teaching 'formal' and 'casual'. I wonder whether the worksheets of the kind that I've seen have mixed up 'formal' with 'correct' and 'casual' with some kind of wrongness . . . I'm genuinely interested in knowing how this is being done.

Question 29

We're back with 'formal' again!

Circle the most formal option in each box below to complete the invitation.

We would like to invite you to a catch-up/celebration/get-together
to mark this fab/really cool/momentous occasion.
It will start up/commence/kick off at 6pm

The most formal sentence (I think!) that comes out of this is: 'We would like to invite you to a celebration to mark this momentous occasion. It will commence at 6pm.'

I'm not sure what is shown or proven by this. I'm not sure why anyone outside of a tiny group of people would want to write to each other like this. Attaching the word 'formal' to it sounds to me like dodging the issue. Writing like this is full of class-based assumptions based on the idea that this way of writing has the same status as say, a piece of formal scientific writing. It doesn't. Writing like this is done in order to flag up a certain class status or an aspiration to acquire the trappings of a particular class status. Formal scientific writing is an agreed code between practitioners going back hundreds of years and is nothing to do with petty 'class' distinctions and everything to do with acquired and learned training.

Actually, I find this question really unpleasant.

Question 32

More stuff on 'formal'! Are they obsessed?

This time it's a matter of micro-distinctions based on dubious categories. Here it is:

Which sentence is the most formal?

She suggested that her mother be present.
She really hopes to be ready on time.
Don't forget to lock the door!
If Johnny's late, we'll start without him.

I've been in this language malarkey for decades. What micro-distinctions are there to be made between sentences 1 and 2 that tell us that the first is 'more formal' than the second? In what ways should this matter or be important or be something that children should spend time learning (or forgetting)? Yes, there are great things to do with register and code-switching, particularly in fiction and when people make speeches. People who write ads do it too. It's great fun for children to experiment with it, in order to see how these people in positions of power do it. Narrowing this down to the kind of distinction that tells us that sentence one is supposedly 'more formal' than sentence two, seems to me to be absurd, all the more so given that I'm not clear that the examiners or anyone else has a clear definition of what is 'formal'. Why, for example, would the formation 'suggest that her mother be' be more formal than 'really hopes to be'? The first sounds to my ears as being a bit more old-fashioned, not more 'formal'.

I suspect that this is an example of grammarians straying into the world of literature and ending up tied in knots. It happens.

Question 39

What is the grammatical term for the underlined word in the sentence below?

My prize was a <u>fluffy, green pencil case with a gold zip</u>.

As I went through this test paper, I was seriously trying to answer the questions. I got to this one and thought that I knew the answer according to the 'grammar' that these examiners believe in. When I was at school, I was taught two things: after the verb 'to be' you get what they call a 'complement'. It's in the glossary (though expressed in a particularly opaque, difficult way.) But I was also taught that all 'verb phrases' are followed by the 'predicate'. So I sat and looked at this and wondered which of these two 'grammatical terms' would be right.

In fact, it's neither! Hooray. It's supposed to be 'expanded noun phrase' or 'noun phrase'. Perhaps I haven't understood the phrase:

'grammatical term'. Who knows! And what possible use is it that I'm wrong when both my answers are in fact right? Agreed that 'predicate' is not in the glossary but maybe one or two keen 10/11 year olds figured that this phrase is a 'complement'. Hard luck on them.

Question 41 is about 'direct speech' and therefore about 'indirect speech' too. I looked for a definition for these in the glossary. They're not there. Why not?

Question 49 uses the term 'present progressive'. Again, for decades we called this the 'present continuous' which had the advantage of using a word – 'continuous' which suggested continuous action. It kind of worked, insofar as any of these terms 'work'. Then someone got paid to turn this into the 'progressive'. Why? To what purpose? Why was 'continuous' replaced? Is it to make older teachers feel redundant and confused? Why is 'progressive' better than 'continuous'? I suggest a game: invent new terms for the old terms and come up with any old justification for why it should be the new term.

More seriously, of course the great industry of worksheets and textbooks don't and can't keep up with this nonsense, so quite often they are 'wrong'. You and your children are supposed to find a way through this jungle. When we remember that it is the teachers being tested here (see Bew Report 2011 for why this is a method of assessment of teachers not pupils) this kind of verbal monkeying has serious consequences.

One last thought. All this effort focuses on one narrow and distorted use of language: 'sentence grammar'. We do not write or talk purely or only in sentence grammar. We write in sequences of sentences and can, if we choose, to not write sentences as with adverts, songs, poems, film scripts, plays and in some cases in stories and novels. When we write we write sequences and passages of language that express meaning across much more than 'sentences'. This too has a grammar (or grammars) of sorts – as expressed by cohesion, prosody, narratology (i.e., looking at how writing is put together across whole passages and stories etc.), rhetoric, pragmatics (where there is dialogue), stylistics and genre.

But even this description misses out the huge area of how we talk to each other! How we talk to each other is a hugely wonderful, complex matter, full of variation and culture. It mostly through this that we define who we are, how we live and think, how we relate to each other. What model of language is it, that leaves this out and restricts education in language to these stilted, invented sentences? Whatever it is, it's false.

Part 6

Open Letter to the Secretary of State for Education

Once a month in *The Guardian*, I write an 'open letter' to the Secretary of State for Education. I've been doing this since the days when Michael Gove was in that job. Here is a recent one about libraries and reading for pleasure.

How strange that prisons have to have a library but schools do not . . .

Dear Gavin Williamson

Did you see the report on school libraries that came out last week? The headline facts are worrying, don't you think?

Schools with a higher proportion of children on free school meals are more than twice as likely not to have access to a designated library space. One in eight schools has no library at all.

And employment terms for librarians and library staff fall below national standards, with low pay and little investment in professional development and training.

The first of these points is a familiar one. It's as if there's some law or commandment which stipulates that children who come from homes with the least money should go to the schools with the least money, too. The employment standards problems are also worrying: they suggest that there is no commitment from government that the specialised knowledge and practice of librarians is a priority.

I've been round this block many times before. I even met your schools minister, Nick Gibb, to discuss how we might all cooperate to foster reading for pleasure. He seemed to be in complete agreement that reading for pleasure was a key element in helping children access the curriculum.

It's not a mystery as to why or how this happens. Children who know how to browse and choose books, and who read widely and often, are immersed in what we might call the strategies of continuous prose. This is a form of language very different from everyday conversation, and to 'get' it needs loads of practice reading and writing.

Reading a lot also creates a body of knowledge of both a 'how' and a 'what'. The how is how writing builds scenes, makes points, unfolds and concludes. The 'what' is the emotions, facts, principles and ideas we meet as we read. This is a reservoir of knowledge and understanding children will draw on as they encounter the curriculum.

If you want to check up on what I'm saying here, I provided Nick Gibb with some research from Mariah Evans et al from the University of Nevada on the benefits for children of being exposed to many books.

If children don't have books at home, where are they going to find them? It is 'kinda obvious', as my children would say: libraries. It's also obvious to me that compulsion from the state is needed here.

One of the curiosities of life is that schools are not obliged to have libraries, but prisons are. Step one, then, is to make it compulsory for schools, too. This has to be backed up with step two: ring-fenced money to support schools' libraries, along with the hiring and training of librarians.

Before you object to such state nannying, I should remind you that on a related matter, the government did find ring-fenced money to support reading. They put in place the phonics screening check at the end of year 1 and created a fund to subsidise, at a rate of 50%, schools' purchase of the phonics resources that the government approved of.

Interestingly, though children have a very high success rate when they are five and six at 'decoding' words (knowing how to say them), when it comes to the tests when they're 10 and 11 and have to show that they understand what they're reading, the scores are not so high.

Can this be because many children are not spending time immersed in reading, building that 'reservoir' I mentioned? I think so. We urgently need libraries and librarians in all schools, for all our children.

Yours,

Michael Rosen

Bibliography

Some Reader-Response titles especially in relation to education:

The Dynamics of Literary Response by Norman N. Holland

Where Texts and Children Meet, eds Eve Bearne and Victor Watson

The Social Construction of Meaning, Reading Literature In Urban Classrooms, by John Yandell [secondary]

The Reading Environment, Aidan Chambers

Reading and Response, eds Michael Hayhoe and Stephen Parker

Talking, Listening, Learning, Effective Talk In The Primary Classroom by Debra Myhill, Susan Jones, Rosemary Hopper

How Texts Teach What Readers Learn, Margaret Meek

What is Poetry? The Essential Guide to Reading and Writing Poems, Michael Rosen

Creativity in Language and Literature, the State of the Art, edited by Joan Swann, Rob Pope Ronald Carter

Readers, Texts, Teachers, Bill Corcoran and Emrys Evans

POETRY AND STORIES FOR PRIMARY AND LOWER SECONDARY SCHOOLS

MICHAEL ROSEN

This is a short guide for teachers on how to teach poetry – reading, responding and writing. It is full of ideas on where and how to start, descriptions of why it's such a valuable activity. It's for you to use, adapt and change as you think best for the school and students you have in front of you.

WHY WRITE? WHY READ?

MICHAEL ROSEN

This booklet gathers together some recent talks and blogs on writing and reading, for use by teachers, librarians, parents, or anyone interested in engaging children and students in reading, writing, analysing why and how we do both.

This booklet is third in a series about reading, writing and responding to literature. It focusses on how to make writing pleasurable and interesting and would be ideal as part of teacher training, staff discussion, curriculum development or just reading and using.

Full details of this series of booklets, along with all my other books, can be found at:

michaelrosen.co.uk/books/

I often post thoughts on education, literature, and current affairs on my blog at: **michaelrosenblog.blogspot.co.uk**

You can also follow my work at: **michaelrosen.co.uk**

CPSIA information can be obtained
at www.ICGtesting.com
Printed in the USA
BVHW031645080321
601998BV00007B/868